ENHANCING 360-DEGREE FEEDBACK FOR SENIOR EXECUTIVES

How to Maximize the Benefits and Minimize the Risks

ENHANCING 360-DEGREE FEEDBACK FOR SENIOR EXECUTIVES

How to Maximize the Benefits and Minimize the Risks

Robert E. Kaplan
Charles J. Palus

Center for Creative Leadership
Greensboro, North Carolina

The Center for Creative Leadership is an international, nonprofit educational institution founded in 1970 to foster leadership and effective management for the good of society overall. As a part of this mission, it publishes books and reports that aim to contribute to a general process of inquiry and understanding in which ideas related to leadership are raised, exchanged, and evaluated. The ideas presented in its publications are those of the author or authors.

The Center thanks you for supporting its work through the purchase of this volume. If you have comments, suggestions, or questions about any Center publication, please contact Bill Drath, Publication Director, at the address given below.

Center for Creative Leadership
Post Office Box 26300
Greensboro, North Carolina 27438-6300

CENTER FOR CREATIVE LEADERSHIP®

CCL No. 160

Library of Congress Cataloging-in-Publication Data

Kaplan, Robert E.
    Enhancing 360-degree feedback for senior executives : how to maximize the benefits and minimize the risks / Robert E. Kaplan, Charles J. Palus.
        p.   cm.
    "CCL no. 160"—T.p. verso.
    Includes bibliographical references.
    ISBN 0-912879-98-X
    1. Executives—Rating of—Methodology. 2. Feedback (Psychology). 3. Employees—Attitudes. 4. Self-evaluation. 5. Executives—Counseling of. I. Palus, Charles J. II. Title.
    HF5549.5.R3K36   1994
    658.4'07125—dc20   94-23151
                                                                         CIP

Table of Contents

Acknowledgments

We would like to thank the following people for their helpful input: Pat Alexander, Barry Berglund, Marilyn Butterfield, David DeVries, Susan Dorn, Bill Drath, Rebecca Henson, Fred Kiel, Connie McArthur, Cindy McCauley, Marie McKee, Eric Rimmer, Sharon Rogolsky, Jeff Staggs, Joan Tavares, Amy Webb, Randy White, Martin Wilcox, and Kathryn Williams.

Preface

In our development work with senior executives, we often make use of a tool that we refer to in this paper as *enhanced 360-degree feedback*. Because of its power, a key issue in its implementation is informed choice. That is, we believe that everyone taking part in such feedback—the executive, the executive's superior, the human resources representative, family, and the staff of the service provider—must be aware in advance of the possible benefits and risks of participation. The HR representative plays a central role—not only choosing the service providers who offer enhanced feedback and selecting the executives who participate but also in helping others make informed choices—and so we have primarily addressed that group in this paper. We do think, however, that what we say here can also be of benefit to other participants.

What we have written, of course, bears the slant of our own experiences with, and interpretations of, particular versions of these methods. Nonetheless, we have tried to approach enhanced feedback as an emerging general class of development interventions for senior managers. This class of intervention is characterized by greater power that seems to be needed to bring about appreciable, sustainable improvements in the leadership exerted by senior executives. (They don't become perfect executives; just better ones.) But to employ that heightened power to good effect requires a very active, conscientious engagement by the key players at critical junctures. This report describes the nature of that engagement.

Introduction

In the past few years, management development has increasingly involved 360-degree feedback—an experience in which a person receives, in anonymous form, ratings of performance from peers, superiors, and subordinates; compares these with self-ratings; and perhaps gets limited coaching and sets goals for improvement. It aims to improve performance by providing a better awareness of strengths and weaknesses, and if the person is experiencing problems, it can be used to develop a more precise understanding of them and what to do in response.

In general, 360-degree feedback is viewed as an effective development technique for all levels of management. Senior executives, however, sometimes require a richer feedback experience. We have worked for many years with programs offering such an experience, which we refer to here as *enhanced 360-degree feedback* or *enhanced feedback.*[1]

Enhanced feedback, in addition to the features mentioned above, also offers some or all of the following: detailed verbatim descriptions; observations from family members and friends; psychometric measures of personality and motivation; data on early, including family, history; and an extended coaching relationship with one or more professionals in leadership development.

Why do senior executives sometimes need more than standard 360-degree feedback? From one perspective, it is because they face a much broader range of challenges than other managers and executives. In addition, based on our research (Kaplan, 1990, 1991; Kaplan, Drath, & Kofodimos, 1991), we believe that there is another factor: the psychological makeup of people who rise to high-level positions. Executives are often extremely achievement-oriented, very forceful, and highly demanding. But such qualities can backfire. Executives can underperform or, perhaps even more serious, get outstanding results in the short run by sacrificing the organization's ability to maintain high performance in the long run.

Standard feedback does not address performance at the psychological level, focusing rather on modifying behavior alone; and little help is given to

---

[1] The programs we have worked with are APEX® and LeaderChange®. APEX® is offered by the Center for Creative Leadership. LeaderChange® is offered by Kaplan DeVries, Inc. A third program that provides enhanced feedback is New Foundations, offered by KRW Inc. Other programs that make use of what may be viewed as enhanced 360-degree feedback are the ICE program of Personnel Decisions, Inc., and the Leadership at the Peak program of the Center for Creative Leadership.

the person in actually applying the results. Also, standard feedback does not typically deal with the general skepticism in organizations about the ability of executives to change on the psychological level. In our work we have found that powerful forces seem to hold them more or less in place. Senior executives are successful people; not surprisingly, they are often reluctant to tamper with what got them to where they are. And whatever their problems may be, they are, by virtue of their high position if not also the contributions they make, treated daily in ways that suggest strongly that they are exceptional and shouldn't need to change (Kaplan, Drath, & Kofodimos, 1985). Enhanced 360-degree feedback, because of its scope and power, provides a way of dealing with such resistance.

Yet its power is also potentially harmful. We have not witnessed any case in which permanent harm was caused by this type of feedback, but we believe that certain standards should be adopted, certain procedures followed, and certain precautions taken to minimize the risk.[2]

The purpose of this paper, then, is to lay out the potential advantages and hazards of enhanced feedback. It is intended primarily for human resources managers who are responsible for the development of executives. HR managers are key because they are in a strong position to ensure good practice. They are responsible for deciding who participates; they select the service provider; they oversee the activity; and they have a role to play as coaches.

In the remainder of this paper we will look at enhanced feedback and its rationale in greater detail; provide evidence and examples of potential benefits and risks; and suggest guidelines for making safe and effective use of it.

A Closer Look at Enhanced Feedback

Enhanced feedback goes beyond standard 360-degree feedback on two counts—in the amount and the type of data collected and in its emphasis on implementation.

---

[2] Standards of ethical practice have been articulated for professionals working with individuals in organizational settings (*American Psychologist*, 1992; Gellerman, Frankel, & Ladenson, 1990; Pope & Vasquez, 1991; Van Hoose & Kottler, 1985). Taking these standards seriously means assessing both the short- and long-term positive as well as potentially negative impacts of each method; it means "informing the people with whom we work about . . . purposes and goals . . . anticipated outcomes, limitations, and risks . . . in a way that supports their freedom of choice in activities initiated by us" (Gellerman et al., 1990, p. 168).

Sources of Data

There are four sources of data in enhanced feedback: numerical ratings plus verbatim comments; data from the workplace plus data from personal life; data on behavior plus data on motivation; and data on the present plus data on early history.

Numerical ratings plus verbatim comments. Numerical, scale-based ratings tend to leave recipients wondering what some of the numbers mean. This is even more true when, as is usually the case, the ratings come from an off-the-shelf instrument; often the person is unclear as to how the generic items apply to him or her in particular. Comments in their co-workers' own words add an extra dimension. The two types of data used in tandem are potent because—if the results on each tell a similar story, and they usually do—the message comes through clearly.

Comments can be gathered using interviews or open-ended questions that co-workers respond to in writing. A drawback of using verbal comments is that, even when they are reported back anonymously, the recipient may be able to identify who said what.

Data from the workplace plus data from personal life. It is common for a person to exhibit similar behavior at home and at work—for instance, holding onto control or planning everything to the *n*th degree. When feedback indicates that this is the case, the person is less likely to deny a behavior. Of course, there are usually also differences in behavior, but these too are instructive.

The way to gather data on personal life is to, in addition to interviewing the executive, talk to family members and, perhaps, friends. This is unusual for a management-development activity and extreme care must be exercised.

Data on behavior plus data on motivation. We believe that if executives are to modify their behavior, they must consider what drives that behavior. This is where the psychological makeup of the person comes in. To be sure, one's psychological makeup is not readily amenable to change—and that is a good thing—but neither is it completely immutable. At a minimum it helps the cause of development if the executive is able to factor in the personal, emotional, inner side of his or her leadership. How to do this? One way is to do a battery of psychological tests. Another way is to collect data on what other people feel is the individual's motivation.

Data on the present plus data on early history. Another way to understand the executive's psychological makeup is to look into his or her past. The principle here is simple: The child continues to live in the adult. One need only ask commonsense questions about an individual's parents, siblings, family life, friends, performance in school, play, and so on, and the likely formative influences emerge fairly clearly. There is always more to learn about the connection between one's past and the present, and the typical executive has not given this much thought. One way to gather information on childhood is to talk with the executive. It also helps to interview members of his or her original family and a childhood friend or two.

Choosing suitable sources. Not all the sources of data described above need to be used in every case. Taking basic 360-degree feedback as the given, the service provider, the HR representative, and the executive should choose carefully what supplementary data sources to add. This will depend on the needs of the executive and the organization and on available resources.

With respect to benefit and risk, the more high-quality data and the more different types of data, the greater the potential impact, in both a positive and a negative sense. Even a basic 360-degree-feedback instrument carries a risk. In general, the greater the impact and more issues potentially raised, the greater the responsibility the provider has to the recipient.

To highlight both the potential risks as well as the potential benefits of enhanced 360-degree feedback to executives, we are concentrating in this paper on the several data sources taken together. The power of such an intervention derives from how much data are fed back. One executive, who had received enhanced feedback and who, because he was in some difficulty organizationally, had received a higher proportion of negative feedback from his co-workers, remarked that the experience was "like having fifty performance appraisals at once." The intervention's impact also derives from the wide variety of data, which raises a range of basic issues—job and career, work and family, present and past, behavior and motivation. The effect is to virtually flood the executive with data. As another executive observed after getting his report, "If you collect enough data on any phenomenon, the basic patterns will pop out. In this work there is no need to hunt and peck for meaning."

For any adult to change, that person must first "unfreeze" (Schein, 1968). These methods tend to loosen up old patterns so that they might be adapted. The data stir up executives, cognitively and emotionally, in the sense they cause them to reconsider their established view of themselves. To one degree or another, the data is unsettling. And in this unsettled state is contained the potential for growth and the potential for harm.

Follow-through

Enhanced feedback differs from standard 360-degree feedback not only in the type and amount of data it provides but also in its emphasis on follow-through. Follow-through serves as a safety measure because it keeps the executive from being left hanging. And it serves as a vital mechanism for helping him or her to translate insight into action.

We provide a detailed discussion on follow-through below (under the subhead "Tide the Executive Through" in the section on "Making Safe Use of Enhanced Feedback").

Possible Outcomes

We are at present conducting two kinds of formal research on the effects of enhanced 360-degree feedback. First, we have done overall evaluations, two or more years after the initial feedback, that assess the changes (if any) that have occurred during that period. Four such studies have been conducted thus far. Second, we have done developmental studies in which we take periodic readings as the process of change unfolds. Five such studies are currently underway. As with the original research that led to this approach to executive development (Kaplan, 1991, pp. 57-58; Kaplan, Drath, & Kofodimos, 1991, pp. 243-246), this is action-research—the data are used both for research purposes and for the benefit of the client. In addition to formal research, we have logged over a twelve-year period a great deal of practical experience using this approach.

Evidence of Gain

What are the chances of bringing about actual improvement in executives using enhanced feedback? The chances appear to be good that executives can make modest, yet nonetheless significant, changes in behavior. The changes make a difference because the insights are *internalized*. In our view, these changes are accompanied by an internal shift that leads the individual and others to feel that the changes are real—not cosmetic—and likely to last. This is the crucial test: Do participants, and the people who know them, feel the differences are authentic? Consider one executive's reflection: "I heard [in the feedback] that I needed to behave differently. What I found after the next few weeks was there was a side of me that hadn't found a place in business. I needed to unlock that place. Rather than merely *act* differently— that would have been shallow—I had to *be* different."

One development need that we typically encounter in executives, even those who are in good standing, is the necessity to be less forceful. One such individual was described as an "elemental force of nature." In our view, the problem comes when they become too "expansive"—too big a personality, too aggressive or controlling or forceful in pursuit of objectives, too willing to work extremely long hours and to expect the same of others, too impressed with their own expertise and knowledge and not receptive enough to inputs from others, too ambitious for themselves, too ambitious for their organizations (Kaplan, 1991). The list could go on.

Tim Foley (not his real name) is an executive who, over a period of several years and with the impetus of enhanced feedback, moderated his overly expansive style and temperament. Hardworking, hard-driving, and hard-edged in his dealings with people, he had been someone who, according to a superior, "got great results but nobody was here to play tomorrow." In a revisit in which we interviewed twenty of his co-workers three years after the feedback, the rating of his effectiveness on a ten-point scale went up two points. The reason: He was no longer so rough on people and he was more inclined to give them the freedom they needed to do their jobs. The perception of the change in his behavior was accompanied by a sense of an inner change. People remarked that he seemed to have "mellowed" somewhat, that he was "more at ease with himself." This corresponded to Foley's own sense that he had grown more confident and therefore no longer needed to grip the reins so tightly—although he was still intensely results-oriented. He was a force that top management felt it could count on for results, but in tempering his style, he did less damage in obtaining those results and in fact increased his productivity by giving his subordinates a greater opportunity to contribute.

Also figuring in the change he made was a new assignment in a completely different part of the company. He took this right after the feedback and was able to start with a clean slate. To cap this, he received a coveted promotion that, according to top management, he would not have received if he had not changed. The outcomes were inspiring but the experience of change was not without discomfort. In the month or two after the feedback, Foley said he felt "as if his fingertips had been sanded down" to the point of painful self-consciousness.

In our experience with enhanced feedback, the chances increase that executives are able to improve their performance at work because they truly internalize the need for change. A subset of the participants actually achieve what we term a *character shift* (Kaplan, 1990). A person's psychological makeup is durable, but this kind of intervention is potent enough to open up the possibility of a modest change—not a total change but rather a partial realignment of one's inner world. What shifts is the executive's values—what the individual deems important versus unimportant, his or her pattern of emotional investments, what he or she puts energy into.

Evidence of Pain

In the years that we have been associated with enhanced feedback, involving dozens of executives, we know of only two individuals, one of whom we will call Brian Haley, who seemed to have been adversely affected by this activity. But our own experience aside, the fact remains that negative outcomes are well within the realm of possibility. It is critical then that anyone considering enhanced feedback make sure that great care is taken in delivering it.

Learning is often painful, and there is no getting around the fact that enhanced feedback has a certain abrasive action that can hurt. Brian Haley clearly benefited from the experience but he was more distressed by it and stayed unsettled longer than most recipients.

Just before receiving the feedback, he was promoted. He had very much wanted the promotion but, in contrast to the happy coincidence of Tim Foley's promotion, the timing interacted badly with the feedback.

A high-potential upper-level manager in his early forties, Haley saw himself as CEO material (a view shared by others) and was chronically impatient for the next promotion. Perhaps because he was precocious, he had a tendency to get ahead of himself and so had always felt insecure during the first few months in a new job. Previously, he had been able to suppress the anxiety and actually to turn it into a redoubled effort to do well. In this case his insecurity in the new job was compounded by the "bad grades" he got in the feedback report.

Another factor was Haley's burning need to perform well and his corresponding fear of not doing so. Life for him was, in many ways, a performance. He turned meetings, especially with his own staff, into a stage on which he could perform, and even in conversations there was a sense of him as not natural because he seemed to be putting on a performance. He was, he came to realize, constantly concerned with impressing people. He was, in fact, impressive in many ways. He was, for example, an exceptional speaker, one of the best in top management—a favorite with investment analysts. But, ironically, his need to impress was a trait that ultimately marred his image.

As bright, knowledgeable, visionary, articulate, hardworking, and polished as he was, he lost credibility by seeming to be overly committed to his own advancement and overly concerned with impressing his superiors. He also seemed to overrely on his own abundant natural talent and, therefore, did not pay enough attention to other people's ideas, especially those of his peers. That his image turned out to be marred at a time when he was feeling insecure in his job proved distressing to Haley.

Two years later, another survey showed that these tendencies had decreased. There was still room for improvement, but Haley was rated as significantly higher on items like "team player," "effective with peers," "empathy," and "putting the organization's goals ahead of his own." The rating of his overall effectiveness as a manager had also gone up. One way to construe the change was that he had become more of a real person, less identified with an image of perfection. At home this was evident in his greater willingness to talk with his wife about his feelings, including the things that bothered him. And it was clear that the reason he had been able to do better was that he had taken the first set of results to heart.

Brian Haley managed in the end to grow and improve but not without significant pain. Once it became apparent, two months after the feedback session, that he was in some distress—and it was not evident in the feedback session—the key was: How would he cope?

Fundamentally, he fell back on his own resources, a considerable resiliency and ego strength that made it possible for him to recognize immediately that he was under stress. Haley gets particular credit for this because he was not deterred by his customary distaste for having problems. Whereas he once had kept problems to himself, in this case he reached out to other people. He turned to his spouse in a way that he never had previously in their fifteen-year marriage. As a result of having personal conversations they did not usually have, the marriage took on an extra measure of closeness.

Haley also turned to his friends and was relieved to discover that some of them had had their own similar struggles. He sought out an expert in stress management and followed that person's advice to get more exercise and to meditate. And he turned to us. Haley's wife said later, "You 'hovered' and that was very important."

We did many things to support him. For instance, we helped him see what his distress meant. By reconstructing recent episodes, he could see that the distress stemmed from being afraid that his "act" was crumbling or was in danger of crumbling. So the outbreak of anxiety proved to be a chance for him to open his eyes to how much he had been ruled by performance anxiety. We helped him to look upon the distress as an opportunity to know himself better and to grow.

Absorbing the Impact

Our experience is that most executives receive enhanced feedback without undue difficulty. For a few weeks they engage in much more introspection than usual, and they have more conversations about themselves than usual. They are self-aware to the point of being self-conscious. Yet for most participants the stress generated by the mass of data is manageable and almost entirely beneficial and growth-producing. In 1991 we surveyed thirty-six individuals who had participated in this activity at the Center for Creative Leadership from 1986 to 1990. We also interviewed the spouses of several participants. The data turned up no evidence of a serious negative outcome.

Making Safe Use of Enhanced Feedback

For HR managers whose responsibility is to help executives with performance problems, a major challenge is: How can a person's weaknesses be alleviated without sacrificing strengths? (This challenge is acute for executives who consistently get outstanding bottom-line results but who do a lot of damage in the process.) Enhanced feedback can help, but to use it safely and effectively, we believe certain dictates of good practice must be followed. First, the best general strategy is, obviously, to choose a service provider with a competent, constructive staff. Second, because high-impact feedback may be unsuitable for a certain percentage of executives, it is critical that participants be carefully selected. Third, to accommodate the fact that participating executives will be unsettled to one degree or another by the heavy dose of feedback, it is vital that staff of the service provider tide participants through the unsettled period.

Select the Right Staff

Feedback is only as good as the staff offering it. The service provider selected should have staff that is: competent at management development, proficient at personal development, effective with senior managers, and mature.

To be competent at management development, one must understand the executive's job, the business and institutional context in which executives perform their jobs, and the typical performance problems that executives have. One must also be adept at the behavioral methods for helping them correct performance problems. The emphasis in management development is on cultivating knowledge, skills, and abilities. It is an outer emphasis.

To be proficient at personal development, one must understand personality, identity, basic motivation, and adult development and also be able to help executives grow as human beings—to moderate intensity, overcome inhibitions, get a better perspective on basic beliefs, and become more honest with themselves about their basic drives. This is an inner emphasis.

To be effective with senior executives, a person must be credible to them. This requires one to be assertive enough to hold one's own and capable of matching them intellectually. A peer relationship must be established.

Maturity means that the staff member consistently puts the client's needs ahead of his or her own, has empathy, is accepting, genuinely cares, and is unfailingly constructive. Of the several criteria for an effective staff, this is the one that bears most heavily on the potential for harm. Any indication of ego problems in a staff person—any tendency to be destructive, self-serving, overly ambitious, neglectful—is adequate cause for the HR manager to disqualify the prospective service provider. If ever there was an occasion to check a person's references thoroughly, this is it.

Select the Right Participants

Almost all managers can handle 360-degree feedback as it is generally practiced, and, consequently, little attention is usually paid, or needs to be paid, to screening. Enhanced feedback is a different story. Some executives may not be up to the rigors of what one person called "emotional boot camp," and so it is imperative that real effort be put into screening.

In our experience there are two types of individuals at risk (Kaplan, 1983; Lieberman, Yalom, & Miles, 1973): those who are fragile and those who are highly defensive and rigid. Both types lack the resources to deal effectively with high stress.

Another risk factor, independent of makeup, is disarray in the executive's life. Suitability for an intervention like this is circumstantial as well as personal. A crisis of one kind or another in an executive's private life might make this a bad time to go through an intensive developmental experience. (On the other hand this *could* be an advantageous time if the individual is more open than usual to soul-searching.) Likewise, the destabilizing circumstance may be job-related—if, for example, the executive is in danger of being terminated or demoted. An HR executive who is experienced in using providers of enhanced feedback commented, "I worry more [about possible harm] when the person is in trouble."

An executive should only participate in an exercise this personal and this intensive ("intrusive" one executive called it) if he or she wants to.

Readiness is everything. A former participant spoke about the willingness to experience a certain amount of pain. "Some people are not ready to cope with this process. The positive inducement is not there."

Timing is key. One executive made the following comment: "When you see the power of the [intervention] . . . you say, 'Why didn't I do that earlier?' But the answer is 'Was I ready for it earlier?'"

So the question is, How do you screen out individuals who, because of their psychological makeup or because of their current circumstances, have an instability or potential instability that the feedback could compound and aggravate? We recommend the following three screens: responsible nominations by the organization, informed choice by the executive nominated, and responsible decisions by the service providers.

The organization nominates. Enhanced feedback is not one of those activities that organizations put managers through in droves, and so decisions about who should receive it can be made on a case-by-case basis. Typically, participants are nominated by a higher-level executive, the HR executive, or the top-management team in one of its executive-succession reviews. For the nominators to make good decisions, they need to fully understand what the experience entails and what the risk factors are. This is especially important in view of the political realities in many institutions: If an executive is chosen to participate, he or she may not feel truly free to decline. Or if the service provider's program staff later advises against having an executive participate, that individual may lose face. An HR executive who had participated in nominating several people for this activity over the years has developed a sensitivity to these issues. "I'm always thinking, 'Can the person handle this?' I think about this as much as about whether the person will benefit. Picking the right people is nine-tenths of it." Because organizations just starting to use enhanced feedback don't have the benefit of long experience with it, nominators must educate themselves about it so that they can make the best decisions possible about who, and who not, to put forward.

Self-selection. As one HR person said, "This is not something someone should do unless they want to." In other words, participation must be voluntary, even if the idea for the executive to take part comes from someone else.

The job of informing potential candidates is made difficult by the fact that extensive, biographically oriented feedback is outside almost everyone's experience. It is something that has to be experienced to be fully appreciated. Yet there are things that the service provider can do to describe what it is like, and it is important that the service provider—as well as the HR staff—be honest about the power of the intervention and its potential for harm. A corporate user of enhanced feedback advised us to tell people, "There's anger, disruption; it's not for the timid. This takes a lot of courage." The service provider might describe it in the following way. "It's like Outward Bound, very demanding as well as potentially very rewarding. There is risk involved—the developmental equivalent of white water. We staff are experienced guides who fully expect that no one will get badly hurt, but the boat might capsize and the water is cold."

It is also helpful, if possible, for potential participants to talk with executives who have been through the same or a similar experience, preferably with the same staff or the same service provider. Ask the service provider if there are former participants who would be willing to discuss their experience with potential participants. This is a sensitive area, because service providers typically maintain confidentiality about who participates in enhanced feedback. If available, however, the candid reports of peers in one's own organization or from other organizations can assist the executive in making an informed choice.

Another way to support informed choice is to involve the executive's spouse in the decision. First, the spouse should be given an opportunity to read about the process. Second, he or she should be invited to the initial meeting with the program staff. The executive and spouse, once they have been briefed, should be encouraged to make a carefully considered decision about the process in general and about collecting data about their personal life.

It is important that executives in any danger of losing their jobs appreciate the possibility of going through termination plus all this feedback. If the executive, aware of the possibility of outplacement, still wants the program, then the level of risk is probably acceptable. A job threat can actually be an advantage: It can give the executive an extra incentive to learn and change. The organization, however, should commit to standing by the executive for at least a few months after the feedback—to give the person a chance to absorb the impact and to see how he or she responds to the feedback.

We should pause here to raise the issue of who receives the feedback. When a person's performance is evaluated for the purpose of development—as distinct from assessment—it is accepted practice that the ratings be given only to that person and not to his or her organization. This is the policy, for instance, underlying all the programs at the Center for Creative Leadership that offer standard 360-degree feedback: The executive owns the results, and the confidentiality of the results is a priority. The only other person that knows the results is the Center's feedback-giver, who offers some coaching.

In the case of enhanced feedback, confidentiality is also a priority. We believe that only the executive should be given complete detailed results. If the executive chooses, he or she may give certain selected people within the organization (for example an HR representative or the executive's superior, one of whom may be acting as a coach) the leadership results or a summary of those results. Who, in addition to the executive, has access to results is a key issue, and it must be part of informed choice.

The service provider selects. In addition to the executive himself or herself and organizational decision-makers, the staff of the service provider needs to take part in the selection, principally by screening out unsuitable individuals. There are two opportunities to do this. First, when an executive is nominated (let's say by the HR executive), the staff has a chance to question his or her viability for enhanced feedback. Second, during the initial discussions with the executive and with the executive and spouse, the staff has a chance to unearth something about the person or his or her circumstances that would advise against participation.

If, after the organization puts a name forward, the staff develops serious concerns about whether enhanced feedback is right for that person, it is important that they be sensitive to the possible stigmatizing effects of disqualifying the someone. "What, this person can't take it?" can be the organization's disparaging response. For this reason, as few people as possible should know that someone has been nominated until the decision is final. More important, the organization should respect the power of enhanced feedback. As one HR executive commented, "Allowing them to say no is important."

Tide the Executive Through

A risk of enhanced feedback is that the executive will be overwhelmed by the quantity and variety of the data or, more likely, by the quantity and intensity of negative data. Consequently, once someone has decided to participate, then it is the service provider's responsibility to do everything possible to guarantee that he or she has a good experience, principally by helping the person cope effectively with the stress of the feedback. Specifically this means: preparing the executive for the feedback; stressing the positives as well as the negatives in the feedback; never coercing or attacking the executive; staying in touch after the feedback session; helping the participant get closure both conceptually and emotionally; challenging the executive to make real progress; and developing a strong relationship with the executive. The participant's HR staff should use the following guidelines to help them oversee the tiding-through process.

Preparation. If selection is done effectively, then the executive and the spouse have to a large extent been prepared for enhanced feedback. But as one participant emphasized, "You have to make sure that people are primed."

For a participating executive, being primed includes knowing where he or she stands organizationally. If there is a performance problem, especially a career-limiting one, then the people in authority should let the person know that this is one reason that he or she has been recommended for enhanced feedback. The HR manager has a responsibility here to carry the message personally or to arrange for the executive's superior to carry the message. One nominating executive brought up the example of a subordinate who "doesn't empower but thinks he does. He's resisted change, so I recommended enhanced feedback for him. We did prior work to prime him for the kinds of changes he needed to make. If HR had him go through without priming, without having any idea of the inconsistency, he might have rejected the feedback and it could have colored him forever." The principle here is that the organization must let the individual know in advance of the feedback where he or she stands generally and not let the feedback data come as a complete surprise. This is one way to alleviate the possible shock. It is also a way to help the recipient take the data seriously.

In addition to the executive, the spouse needs to be prepared for the role he or she will likely be called on to play. This was the clear message from the spouses we have talked with. One of them made this comment about the feedback process: "I didn't know what to expect. I wasn't prepared. A few months before the session I was told that the spouse was going to be important, but I didn't know what that meant." It is important to avoid creating a situation in which the executive is going through a process of change and the spouse is not—in which "one person has insight and the other doesn't," as one participant put it.

Good preparation then may consist of telling participants, as one HR manager put it, "There will be some bumps in the road."

Stress the positive. It's easy during the feedback session and afterward for everyone to focus on the criticism. Concerned about the executive's development, the service providers or the HR manager and the executive's superior may pay primary attention to what performance problems need correcting. The executive, as is common with achievement-oriented people, may dwell on his or her shortcomings. But even if the participant succumbs to that tendency, the staff should certainly resist it. In going over the data during the feedback session, for example, executives typically turn quickly from the section on strengths to the section on weaknesses. If that happens, the executive should be advised to pause to reflect on and savor the good news. Later when the data are summarized, strengths as well as weaknesses should be emphasized. Again, the HR executive and superior should follow suit.

The reason for paying attention to both strengths and weaknesses is that development depends as much on accepting strengths as it does on recognizing weaknesses. An executive may have heard about the good things before, but it is unlikely that his or her assets, talents, and efficacy have been catalogued and articulated so fully and compellingly. For most executives, then, the positive feedback presents a golden opportunity to realize, "Gee, I'm good!" Also, excessive intensity and ambition, in our view, partly come from underlying doubts about one's worth. So it is important that the executive let the evidence of strengths sink in.

The service provider should never attack or coerce. When executives are defensive—when they resist the data or the full significance of the data—staff must never force him or her to get the message. The stance has to be one of respecting the individual's defenses. If the data don't penetrate the defenses and cause the person to rethink, and if the staff's constructive efforts don't change that, then it is imperative that the staff not attempt to make the executive see the light. It may be that the person never feels able to call assumptions into question. Or it may be that, as has been our experience occasionally, the person will come around months or years later. In any case, no matter how thwarted the staff member may feel, coercion or attack is never an option. Research on another powerful intervention, encounter groups, indicates clearly that the use of force is a chief cause of casualties (Kaplan, 1983).

Staff are most tempted to pressure individuals who, not surprisingly, are very resistant and who, not coincidentally, have serious performance problems. But it must be remembered that such people are actually quite vulnerable and therefore must be treated with particular care.

After the feedback session, make sure that the service provider stays in touch. The service provider must maintain contact with the executive following feedback. A wealth of data is given to the person during feedback, and it is important that he or she be given help in sorting it out. If the person is unsettled, then the staff can help settle him or her down. If the data have revealed difficult problems, the staff should stay actively engaged until all the problems have in some fashion been dealt with. This is one of the highest principles of enhanced feedback. Virtually every client or spouse we talked with about this process stresses the need for follow-up. As one executive expressed it, "There's a window for short-term follow-up in the 'post-operative' period." The more serious the "operation," then, the greater the need for post-operative assistance. Under these conditions, you "hover," to use the term employed by Brian Haley's wife. In addition to the staff of the service provider, other individuals should stay involved—the executive's boss, the appropriate HR executive, and so on. They must take an interest, be available.

The service provider should help the executive get closure. Enhanced feedback yields so much data that it can threaten to overwhelm the recipient, no matter how bright and analytical the person is. Executives need conceptual closure.

One participant exclaimed in the midst of the feedback session: "I'm drowning in data! I need buckets!" He wanted to reduce the data to a few categories of strengths and weaknesses. These categories must be created inductively and not by imposing a preconceived framework. The way we accomplish this is to have the participant and the staff each independently summarize the data and then collaborate in creating a customized set of buckets, as it were.

Another step in helping the executive gain conceptual closure on the data is to define developmental objectives and strategies for attaining their objectives.

In addition, participants need emotional closure. If the post-feedback challenge is to contain the data, it is also to contain the emotions stirred up by the data. Emotional closure comes in part from creating order out of informational chaos. It also comes from helping the executive work through feelings about the disparity between one's sense of oneself versus the perceptions of others—whether the disparity makes for an unpleasant or a pleasant surprise.

Another way that participants can contain all the information and emotions is for them to talk to key individuals in their work lives and private lives about what they are learning about themselves and about what actions they might take. In these various ways they can thus come to terms with the voluminous contents of their developmental biography. The HR manager should also assist in this process.

Challenge the executive to make real progress. Senior managers are usually amply motivated to improve, but it helps if the organization, as represented by the HR manager or the person's boss, challenges the executive to set and achieve important developmental goals. Receiving feedback is not the whole job. A feedback session is merely an activity. It is the outcomes one achieves with the feedback that matter.

For any feedback, standard or enhanced, to succeed, it should be treated as an early step in a process with the same results orientation as any other business undertaking. Accountability is critical. An excellent way to build in accountability is to measure progress. If the executive has made an appreciable change, the people in regular contact with him or her will likely know it and be able to report it—to the HR manager, to the superior, to the service provider, or to the executive himself or herself. This latter-stage feedback will reinforce the executive for progress made and challenge him or her to close any remaining gap. The latter-stage feedback session also serves as another opportunity for the executive to problem-solve and for the others involved to coach. If sustainable improvement is what the organization wants, then it is essential that the executive follow through, and it is incumbent on the HR manager to arrange for him or her to do so.

Make sure that the service provider builds a strong relationship with the client. Throughout the process and especially during the unsettled period following feedback, the service provider's relationship with the client, as we have been suggesting, is key. Although the large quantity of data is necessary to the process of change, by itself it is not sufficient. To withstand the rigors of the feedback, the executive needs from the service provider's staff, in addition to technical assistance, the sure sense that they are there for him or her. The service provider must care.

To care means to provide moral support—reassurance of the individual's value as a manager and as a person. An HR executive observed, "It's unsettling to find yourself in the middle of a stream. You need something to stand on. So the availability of support is key. What does support look like? It's not: 'Here, I'll take you out of your pain.' Instead: 'I'll help you work with it.' Being available and having a sense of humor are indispensable." Emotional support for someone hit hard by negative data is especially important.

To care also means to have empathy for what the individual is experiencing. Empathy helps not only because it supports but also because it informs. With empathy, the staff is more likely to detect distress signals that may not be apparent to a detached observer.

Again, caring is not the responsibility only of the service provider's staff. It is important for key individuals surrounding the executive to show that they care by taking a personal interest in what he or she is learning and going through. It is essential that the HR manager get involved in this way.

Conclusion

The key to minimizing the risk in using enhanced feedback is to reduce uncertainty: uncertainty about who is being put forward to participate in it; uncertainty in the prospective participant's mind about what it involves; and uncertainty about how the staff of the service provider will respond under pressure. For this reason, it is best if enhanced feedback is regularly used in an organization so that both the staff of the organization and the staff of the service provider build up an experience base with it and with each other. The first time an organization has one of its executives participate, extra care must be taken to educate nominators and potential participants about enhanced feedback and to educate the service provider's staff about the organization and the potential participants.

This challenging feedback-and-development process can be used to achieve lasting improvements in the way executives lead, provided that the key HR managers do their part. This includes making the basic decision, with other senior leaders of the organization, about whether a service of this intensity and impact is right for the organization. It also includes making carefully considered case-by-case decisions in which possible participants are given the opportunity to decline this experience. And it includes getting involved directly and indirectly to support each executive who chooses to participate.

If the necessary precautions are taken, then most executives can gain a heightened awareness, well beyond what most awareness-raising exercises create, of their impact. They can also gain incentive to do something about whatever problems come to light. Executives thus can be able to be more honest with themselves, to accept the good news and the bad news, including their motives for behaving the way they do. The payoff is typically a change that is internalized. What enhanced feedback does is to stimulate the natural processes of development by focusing attention on issues that might later come to a head on their own.

19

Bibliography

American Psychologist. (1992). Ethical principles of psychologists. *American Psychologist, 45,* 390-395.

Gellerman, W., Frankel, M. S., & Ladenson, R. F. (1990). *Values and ethics in organization and human systems development: Responding to dilemmas in professional life.* San Francisco: Jossey-Bass.

Kaplan, R. E. (1983). The perils of intensive management training and how to avoid them. *Professional Psychology, 14,* 756-770.

Kaplan, R. E. (1990). *Character shifts: The challenge of improving executive performance through personal growth.* Greensboro, NC: Center for Creative Leadership.

Kaplan, R. E. (1991). *The expansive executive* (2nd ed.). Greensboro, NC: Center for Creative Leadership.

Kaplan, R. E., Drath, W. H., & Kofodimos, J. R. (1985). *High hurdles: The challenge of executive self-development.* (Technical Report No. 125). Greensboro, NC: Center for Creative Leadership.

Kaplan, R. E., Drath, W. H., & Kofodimos, J. R. (1991). *Beyond ambition: How driven managers can lead better and live better.* Reading, MA: Addison-Wesley.

Lieberman, M. A., Yalom, I. D., & Miles, M. B. (1973). *Encounter groups: First facts.* New York: Basic Books.

Pope, K. S., & Vasquez, M. J. T. (1991). *Ethics in psychotherapy and counseling: A practical guide for psychologists.* San Francisco: Jossey-Bass.

Schein, E. H. (1968). Brainwashing. In W. G. Bennis, E. H. Schein, & F. I. Steele (Eds.), *Interpersonal dynamics* (Rev. ed., pp. 406-426). Homewood, IL: Dorsey.

Van Hoose, W. H., & Kottler, J. A. (1985). *Ethical and legal issues in counseling and psychotherapy: A comprehensive guide* (2nd ed.). San Francisco: Jossey-Bass.

CENTER FOR CREATIVE LEADERSHIP PUBLICATIONS

SELECTED REPORTS:

Beyond Work-Family Programs J.R. Kofodimos (1995, Stock #167) $25.00

CEO Selection: A Street-Smart Review G.P. Hollenbeck (1994, Stock #164) $25.00

Character Shifts: The Challenge of Improving Executive Performance Through Personal Growth R.E. Kaplan (1990, Stock #143) $30.00

Coping With an Intolerable Boss M.M. Lombardo & M.W. McCall, Jr. (1984, Stock #305) $10.00

The Creative Opportunists: Conversations with the CEOs of Small Businesses J.S. Bruce (1992, Stock #316) $12.00

Creativity in the R&D Laboratory T.M. Amabile & S.S. Gryskiewicz (1987, Stock #130) $12.00

The Dynamics of Management Derailment M.M. Lombardo & C.D. McCauley (1988, Stock #134) $12.00

Eighty-eight Assignments for Development in Place: Enhancing the Developmental Challenge of Existing Jobs M.M. Lombardo & R.W. Eichinger (1989, Stock #136) $15.00

Enhancing 360-degree Feedback for Senior Executives: How to Maximize the Benefits and Minimize the Risks R.E. Kaplan & C.J. Palus (1994, Stock #160) $15.00

An Evaluation of the Outcomes of a Leadership Development Program C.D. McCauley & M.W. Hughes-James (1994, Stock #163) $35.00

The Expansive Executive (Second Edition) R.E. Kaplan (1991, Stock #147) $25.00

Feedback to Managers, Volume I: A Guide to Evaluating Multi-rater Feedback Instruments E. Van Velsor & J. Brittain Leslie (1991, Stock #149) $20.00

Feedback to Managers, Volume II: A Review and Comparison of Sixteen Multi-rater Feedback Instruments E. Van Velsor & J. Brittain Leslie (1991, Stock #150) $80.00

Gender Differences in the Development of Managers: How Women Managers Learn From Experience E. Van Velsor & M. W. Hughes (1990, Stock #145) $35.00

High Hurdles: The Challenge of Executive Self-Development R.E. Kaplan, W.H. Drath, & J.R. Kofodimos (1985, Stock #125) $15.00

The Intuitive Pragmatists: Conversations with Chief Executive Officers J.S. Bruce (1986, Stock #310) $12.00

Key Events in Executives' Lives E.H. Lindsey, V. Homes, & M.W. McCall, Jr. (1987, Stock #132) $65.00

Leadership for Turbulent Times L.R. Sayles (1995, Stock #325) $20.00

Learning How to Learn From Experience: Impact of Stress and Coping K.A. Bunker & A.D. Webb (1992, Stock #154) $30.00

Making Common Sense: Leadership as Meaning-making in a Community of Practice W.H. Drath & C.J. Palus (1994, Stock #156) $15.00

Off the Track: Why and How Successful Executives Get Derailed M.W. McCall, Jr., & M.M. Lombardo (1983, Stock #121) $10.00

Preventing Derailment: What To Do Before It's Too Late M.M. Lombardo & R.W. Eichinger (1989, Stock #138) $25.00

Readers' Choice: A Decade of *Issues & Observations* W.H. Drath, Editor (1990, Stock #314) $15.00

The Realities of Management Promotion M.N. Ruderman & P.J. Ohlott (1994, Stock #157) $20.00

Redefining What's Essential to Business Performance: Pathways to Productivity, Quality, and Service L.R. Sayles (1990, Stock #142) $20.00

Succession Planning L.J. Eastman (1995, Stock #324) $20.00

Training for Action: A New Approach to Executive Development R.M. Burnside & V.A. Guthrie (1992, Stock #153) $15.00

Traps and Pitfalls in the Judgment of Executive Potential M.N. Ruderman & P.J. Ohlott (1990, Stock #141) $20.00

Twenty-two Ways to Develop Leadership in Staff Managers R.W. Eichinger & M.M. Lombardo (1990, Stock #144) $15.00

Understanding Executive Performance: A Life-Story Perspective C.J. Palus, W. Nasby, & R.D. Easton (1991, Stock #148) $20.00

Upward-communication Programs in American Industry A.I. Kraut & F.H. Freeman (1992, Stock #152) $30.00

Why Executives Lose Their Balance J.R. Kofodimos (1989, Stock #137) $20.00

Why Managers Have Trouble Empowering: A Theoretical Perspective Based on Concepts of Adult Development W.H. Drath (1993, Stock #155) $15.00

SELECTED BOOKS:

Balancing Act: How Managers Can Integrate Successful Careers and Fulfilling Personal Lives J.R. Kofodimos (1993, Stock #247) $27.00

Beyond Ambition: How Driven Managers Can Lead Better and Live Better R.E. Kaplan, W.H. Drath, & J.R. Kofodimos (1991, Stock #227) $29.95

Breaking the Glass Ceiling: Can Women Reach the Top of America's Largest Corporations? (Updated Edition) A.M. Morrison, R.P. White, & E. Van Velsor (1992, Stock #236) $19.95

Choosing to Lead K.E. Clark & M.B. Clark (1994, Stock #249) $35.00

Developing Diversity in Organizations: A Digest of Selected Literature A.M. Morrison & K.M. Crabtree (1992, Stock #317) $25.00

Discovering Creativity: Proceedings of the 1992 International Creativity and Innovation Networking Conference S.S. Gryskiewicz (Ed.) (1993, Stock #319) $30.00

Executive Selection: A Look at What We Know and What We Need to Know D.L. DeVries (1993, Stock #321) $20.00

Healing the Wounds: Overcoming the Trauma of Layoffs and Revitalizing Downsized Organizations D.M. Noer (1993, Stock #245) $26.00

If I'm In Charge Here, Why Is Everybody Laughing? D.P. Campbell (1980, Stock #205) $9.40

If You Don't Know Where You're Going You'll Probably End Up Somewhere Else D.P. Campbell (1974, Stock #203) $8.95

Impact of Leadership K.E. Clark, M.B. Clark, & D.P. Campbell (Eds.) (1992, Stock #235) $59.50

Inklings: Collected Columns on Leadership and Creativity D.P. Campbell (1992, Stock #233) $15.00

Leadership Education 1994-1995: A Source Book F.H. Freeman, K.B. Knott, & M.K. Schwartz (Eds.) (1994, Stock #322) $59.00

Leadership: Enhancing the Lessons of Experience R.L. Hughes, R.C. Ginnett, & G.J. Curphy (1992, Stock #246) $40.95

The Lessons of Experience: How Successful Executives Develop on the Job M.W. McCall, Jr., M.M. Lombardo, & A.M. Morrison (1988, Stock #211) $22.95

Making Diversity Happen: Controversies and Solutions A.M. Morrison, M.N. Ruderman, & M. Hughes-James (1993, Stock #320) $25.00

Measures of Leadership K.E. Clark & M.B. Clark (Eds.) (1990, Stock #215) $59.50

The New Leaders: Guidelines on Leadership Diversity in America A.M. Morrison (1992, Stock #238) $29.00

Performance Appraisal on the Line D.L. DeVries, A.M. Morrison, S.L. Shullman, & M.L. Gerlach (1981, Stock #206) $15.00

Readings in Innovation S.S. Gryskiewicz & D.A. Hills (Eds.) (1992, Stock #240) $25.00

Take the Road to Creativity and Get Off Your Dead End D.P. Campbell (1977, Stock #204) $8.95

Whatever It Takes: The Realities of Managerial Decision Making (Second Edition) M.W. McCall, Jr., & R.E. Kaplan (1990, Stock #218) $30.40

The Working Leader: The Triumph of High Performance Over Conventional Management Principles L.R. Sayles (1993, Stock #243) $24.95

SPECIAL PACKAGES:

Conversations with CEOs (includes 310 & 316) $16.00

Development & Derailment (includes 136, 138, & 144) $30.00

The Diversity Collection (includes 145, 236, 238, 317, & 320) $85.00

Executive Selection Package (includes 141, 321, & 157) $32.00

Feedback to Managers: Volumes I & II (includes 149 & 150) $85.00

Personal Growth, Taking Charge, and Enhancing Creativity (includes 203, 204, & 205) $20.00

Discounts are available. Please write for a comprehensive Publication & Products Catalog. Address your request to: Publication, Center for Creative Leadership, P.O. Box 26300, Greensboro, NC 27438-6300, 910-545-2805, or fax to 910-545-3221. All prices subject to change.

ORDER FORM

Name _____ Title _____

Organization _____

Mailing Address_____
(street address required for mailing)

City/State/Zip _____

Telephone _____ FAX _____
(telephone number required for UPS mailing)

Quantity	Stock No.	Title	Unit Cost	Amount
		Subtotal		
		Shipping and Handling (add 6% of subtotal with a $4.00 minimum; add 40% on all international shipping)		
		All NC Residents add 6% sales tax		
		TOTAL		

METHOD OF PAYMENT

❏ Check or money order enclosed (payable to Center for Creative Leadership).

❏ Purchase Order No. _____ (Must be accompanied by this form.)

❏ Charge my order, plus shipping, to my credit card:
    ❏ American Express ❏ Discover ❏ MasterCard ❏ VISA

ACCOUNT NUMBER: _____ EXPIRATION DATE: MO. ___ YR. ___

NAME OF ISSUING BANK: _____

SIGNATURE _____

❏ Please put me on your mailing list.
❏ Please send me the Center's quarterly newsletter, *Issues & Observations*.

Publication • Center for Creative Leadership • P.O. Box 26300
Greensboro, NC 27438-6300
910-545-2805 • FAX 910-545-3221

Client Priority Code: R

_____

_____

_____

CENTER FOR CREATIVE LEADERSHIP
PUBLICATION
P. O. Box 26300
Greensboro, NC 27438-6300